S0-CJQ-555

MASTERPIECES OF MODERN ART

A Picture Book of

19th and 20th Century Masterpieces

from the Thannhauser Foundation

THE SOLOMON R. GUGGENHEIM MUSEUM

THE SOLOMON R. GUGGENHEIM FOUNDATION

President   Peter O. Lawson-Johnston

Trustees   H. H. Arnason, Eleanor, Countess Castle Stewart,
Joseph W. Donner, Mason Welch Gross, Henry Allen Moe,
A. Chauncey Newlin, Mrs. Henry Obre, Daniel Catton Rich,
Albert E. Thiele, Michael F. Wettach, Carl Zigrosser

THE SOLOMON R. GUGGENHEIM MUSEUM

Director   Thomas M. Messer

Staff   Linda Konheim, Administrative Assistant; Agnes R. Connolly,
Auditor; Susan L. Halper, Secretary.

Louise Averill Svendsen, Curator; Diane Waldman, Curator
of Exhibitions; Margit Rowell, Associate Curator;
Carol Fuerstein, Linda Shearer, Research Fellows;
Mary Joan Hall, Librarian; Penny Koleman, Coordinator.

Orrin Riley, Conservator; Lucy Belloli, Assistant Conservator;
Saul Fuerstein, Preparator; Robert E. Mates, Paul Katz,
Photographers; David Roger Anthony, Registrar;
Dana Cranmer, Coordinator.

Anne B. Grausam, Press Representative; Miriam Emden,
Members' Representative; John P. Rafferty, Book Store Supervisor;
Darrie Hammer, Information; Carolyn Porcelli, Coordinator.

Peter G. Loggin, Superintendent; Guy Fletcher, Jr., Assistant
Superintendent; Charles F. Banach, Head Guard;
Yolanda Bako, Coordinator.

Published by
The Solomon R. Guggenheim Foundation
New York, 1972
© The Solomon R. Guggenheim Foundation, 1972
Library of Congress Card Catalogue
Number, 72-75939
Printed in the United States of America

Preface

In 1963 an agreement was signed among Justin K. Thannhauser, the Thannhauser Foundation and The Solomon R. Guggenheim Foundation, under which seventy-five works—paintings, sculptures, watercolors and drawings—by nineteenth and twentieth-century French masters will ultimately be bequeathed to the Guggenheim Museum. Subsequently, Mr. Thannhauser, through his foundation, arranged for a first showing of a partial selection of these works at the Guggenheim from April to September of 1965. Since then, the entire collection marked for eventual transfer under the bequest agreement, has continuously occupied a separate area within the Museum, and has been enjoyed by thousands of visitors. The extensive use of the reserved premises took its toll, however, resulting in the need for some repair and reinstallation, which, on the recommendation of Thomas M. Messer, the Museum's Director, have been approved by the Guggenheim's Trustees.

There was an additional reason for deciding to reshape the gallery at this time: namely, Justin K. Thannhauser's eightieth birthday on May 7, 1972. To improve the presentation of his masterpieces and to issue a new and revised edition of this accompanying publication seemed to us to be an appropriate gesture of our sincere appreciation. We think it is timely to repeat what my cousin and predecessor in office, the late Harry F. Guggenheim wrote on the occasion of the collection's first public showing: "Our gratitude to Mr. Thannhauser is unbounded. He has not only been a munificent benefactor but also a rare and wise counsellor to whom we are in debt for his friendship and advice . . . . The public of New York, and indeed the world of art, will have the opportunity to enjoy this collection . . . in the new Thannhauser wing of the Museum."

Peter Lawson-Johnston, *President*
The Solomon R. Guggenheim Foundation

Introduction

The earliest work in the Thannhauser bequest, Daumier's *The Chess Players* is dated c. 1863; the most recent, from 1960, is Picasso's *Two Doves with Wings Spread*. Between these, Mr. Thannhauser's gift is comprised of paintings, drawings, watercolors and sculptures ranging from the Impressionist and Post-Impressionist era through periods of twentieth-century French art. This latter phase culminates in a group of thirty-four works by Pablo Picasso which, by itself, would be the envy of any collection concerned with modern painting.

The seventy-five works that make up the Thannhauser bequest to the Guggenheim Museum, in the first instance must be viewed for what they are, that is, apart from art history and irrespective of their place in the Museum's collection as a whole. Such masterpieces as Pissarro's *Les Côteaux de l'Hermitage, Pontoise,* Manet's *Before the Mirror* and *Woman in Evening Dress,* Degas' *Dancer in Repose,* Renoir's *Woman with Parrot (Lise),* Cézanne's *Still Life: Flask, Glass and Jug* and *Bibémus,* van Gogh's *Mountains at Saint-Rémy,* Gauguin's *In the Vanilla Field, Man and Horse* and *Haere Mai,* Toulouse-Lautrec's *Au Salon,* Picasso's *Woman Ironing* and *Woman with Yellow Hair* and Braque's *Landscape near Antwerp,* to mention only the most obvious examples among major paintings, need no conceptual justification, nor does their enjoyment depend upon the categoric framework that art history and the orderly arrangements of museum collections require. Viewed, on the other hand, with such sequential and didactic considerations in mind, the Thannhauser Collection at the Guggenheim Museum falls into two parts divided by the magic year 1900 which, through historical coincidence, is not only a conveniently round number, but a stylistic watershed placed between works that look different because they were created by different generations of artists motivated by different prevailing attitudes.

For the collection of The Solomon R. Guggenheim Museum as a whole, the Impressionist and Post-Impressionist portions of the Thannhauser bequest serve as a point of departure and perhaps as a summary introduction for its habitual concern with twentieth-century art. The

Thannhauser works of the twentieth century, on the other hand, particularly its magnificent sequence of Picassos, run historically and stylistically parallel with what the Guggenheim Museum has collected since its inception. In some instances, the Thannhauser works from this period fill what before were painful voids, in others, they document pleasurably and in greater depth what already exists as part of our institutional heritage. In the all-important case of Picasso, for instance, the Guggenheim's own small collection of thirteen works is dramatically increased to a total number of forty-seven. What is more important, however, than this numerical strengthening, is the enhancement of the Picasso collection's range from its former restriction to various phases of Cubism, to one including choice examples from the early Fauve, Blue and Rose periods, as well as from the Surrealist and late phases of the master. Without such a broadening of scope and scale, Picasso's protean achievement would be conveyed in all too fragmentary a form. Similarly, the addition of a Fauve and a late Braque assumes added significance when related to two important Cubist paintings by the same artist already in the Guggenheim's permanent collection. Soutine and Rouault, on the other hand, are names previously unrepresented and their addition to the collection through outstanding examples in the bequest are of inestimable value.

The collection now lent to us through the courtesy of the Thannhauser Foundation and destined for transfer to the Guggenheim Museum through an eventual bequest, is too rich and varied to be adequately covered in this preliminary volume. Provisions have been made, however, for thorough research of the works comprising it, and for a subsequent, fully documented catalogue publication based on such an effort. In the meantime, the Guggenheim Museum is offering this pictorial record as a guide to Museum visitors.

Thomas M. Messer, *Director*
The Solomon R. Guggenheim Museum

*Works by individual artists are grouped together and listed in date order. The artists,
in general, are listed chronologically according to their birthdates. There is an alphabetical
index at the back of the book.*

1808-1879   HONORÉ DAUMIER

The Chess Players. c. 1863
Oil on canvas, 9⅜ x 12⅞"

1830-1903   CAMILLE PISSARRO

Les Côteaux de l'Hermitage, Pontoise. c. 1867
Oil on canvas, 59½ x 78¾"

1832-1883   EDOUARD MANET

Before the Mirror. 1876
Oil on canvas, 36½ x 28½"

EDOUARD MANET

Woman in Evening Dress. 1878
Oil on canvas, 69¾ x 31½"

1834-1917   EDGAR DEGAS

Dancer Moving Forward, Arms Raised. 1882-95
Bronze, 13¾″ h.
2 views

EDGAR DEGAS

Dancer in Repose. 1897-1900
Pastel on monotype, 21 x 17"

EDGAR DEGAS

Dancers in Green and Yellow (Four Dancers). c. 1903
Pastel on board, 36¾ x 26⅜"

EDGAR DEGAS

Spanish Dance. 1896-1911
Bronze, 16″ h.

EDGAR DEGAS

Seated Woman, Wiping her Left Side. 1896-1911
Bronze, 13⅜″ h.

17

1839-1906   PAUL CÉZANNE

Still Life: Flask, Glass and Jug. c. 1877
Oil on canvas, 18½ x 21¾"

PAUL CÉZANNE

Still Life: Plate of Peaches. 1879-82
Oil on canvas, 23½ x 28⅞″

PAUL CÉZANNE

Madame Cézanne. 1885-87
Oil on canvas, 21¼ x 17"

PAUL CÉZANNE

Bibémus. c. 1900
Oil on canvas, 28 x 35⅜"

1841-1919   PIERRE AUGUSTE RENOIR

Woman with Parrot (Lise). c. 1872
Oil on canvas, 36¼ x 25⅝″

PIERRE AUGUSTE RENOIR

The Algerian. 1883
Oil on canvas, 16½ x 12⅞"

23

1848-1903　PAUL GAUGUIN

Haere Mai. Tahiti, 1891

24　　　　　Oil on burlap, 28½ x 36″

PAUL GAUGUIN

In the Vanilla Field, Man and Horse. Tahiti, 1891
Oil on burlap, 28½ x 36″

PIERRE AUGUSTE RENOIR

Still Life: Flowers. 1885

Oil on canvas, 32 x 25½″

1853-1890   VINCENT VAN GOGH

The Viaduct. c. 1887
Oil on board, 12¾ x 16⅜″

VINCENT VAN GOGH

Letter to John Russell. April 1888

Ink, 8⅛ x 10½"

Rare letter in English

28

I heard Rodin had a beautiful head at the Salon.

I have been to the seaside for a week and very likely am going thither again soon. - Flat shore sands - fine figures there like Cimabue - straight stylish.

Am working at a Sower:

The great field all violet the sky & sun very yellow. It is a hard subject to treat.

Please remember me very kindly to Mrs Russell - and in thought I heartily shake hands.

Yours very truly
Vincent

My dear ▮▮▮ for ever so long I have been wanting to write to you - but then the work has so taken me up. We have harvest time here at present and I am always in the fields.

And when I sit down to write I am so abstracted by recollections of what I have seen that I leave the letter. For instance at the present occasion I was writing to you and going to say something about Arles as it is - and as it was in the old days of Boccaccio. -

Well instead of continuing the letter I began to draw on the very paper the head of a dirty little girl I saw this afternoon whilst I was painting a view of the river with a greenish yellow sky.

This dirty 'mudlark' I thought yet had a vague florentine sort of figure like the heads in the monticelli pictures. and reasoning and drawing this wise I worked on the letter

I was writing to you. I enclose the slip of scribbling. that you may judge of my abstractions and forgive my not writing before as such.

So not however imagine I am painting old florentine scenery - no I may dream of such - but I spend my time in painting and drawing landscapes or rather studies of colour.

The actual inhabitants of this country often remind me of the figures we see in Zola's work.

And Manet would like them as they are and the city as it is?

Bernard is still in Brittany and I believe he is working hard and doing well.

Gauguin is in Brittany too but has again suffered of an attack of his liver complaint. I wished I were in the same place with him or he here with me.

My brother has an exhibition of 10 new pictures by Claude Monet - his latest works. for instance a landscape with red sun set and a group of dark fir trees by the sea side

The red sun casts an orange or blood red reflection on the blue green trees and the ground. I wished I could see them.

How is your house in Brittany getting on and have you been working in the country.

I believe my brother has also another picture by Gauguin which is as I heard say very fine two negro women talking. It is one of those he did at martinique.

Mc Knight told me he had seen at marseilles a picture by monticelli, flowerpiece.

Very soon I intend sending over some studies to you and then you can if you like choose one for our exchange.

I must hurry off this letter for I feel some more abstractions coming on and if I did not quickly fill up my paper I would again set to drawing and you would not have your letter. -

Vincent

VINCENT VAN GOGH

Letter to John Russell (with Drawing of Sower). June-July 1888

Ink, 8¼ x 10¼"

Rare letter in English

29

VINCENT VAN GOGH

Letter to John Russell. January 1890

Ink, 7¾ x 8⅞"

VINCENT VAN GOGH

Boats at Saintes Maries. June 1888

Ink, 9½ x 12⅝″

31

VINCENT VAN GOGH

Head of a Girl. Arles, June-July 1888
Ink, 7 x 7⅝″

VINCENT VAN GOGH

The Road from Tarascon. 1888
Ink, 9½ x 12⅝"

33

VINCENT VAN GOGH

The Zouave. Arles, 1888

Ink, 9½ x 12⅝″

VINCENT VAN GOGH

Mountains at Saint-Rémy. July 1889
Oil on canvas, 29 x 37″

1861-1944   ARISTIDE MAILLOL

Woman with Crab. c. 1900-05
Bronze, 6″ h.

1864-1901   HENRI DE TOULOUSE-LAUTREC

Au Salon. Paris, 1893
Pastel and tempera on board, 20⅜ x 30⅞″

38

67-1940   EDOUARD VUILLARD

Place Vintimille. c. 1908
Tempera on board mounted on canvas,
two panels, each 76 x 25½″

39

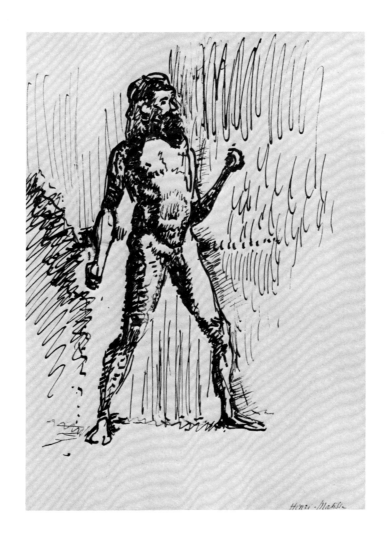

1869-1954   HENRI MATISSE

Male Model. Paris, c. 1900

Ink, 12¼ x 9″

HENRI MATISSE

Woman before Mirror. November 1939
Ink, 15 x 11″

1871-1958   GEORGES ROUAULT

Christ and the Fisherman. c. 1930-40

42   Oil on canvas, 21¼ x 30″

1880-1954   ANDRÉ DERAIN

Still Life: Fruit. c. 1927-28
Oil on canvas, 6⅜ x 13⅞"

43

1881 PABLO PICASSO

The End of the Road. Barcelona, c. 1898
Watercolor and conté crayon, 17⅞ x 11¾"

44

PABLO PICASSO

Le Moulin de la Galette. Paris, 1900
Oil on canvas, 35½ x 46"

45

PABLO PICASSO

Au Café. Madrid, 1901
Charcoal, 7⅞ x 9⅜″

PABLO PICASSO

The Fourteenth of July. Montmartre, 1901
Oil on board mounted on canvas, 19 x 24⅞″

47

PABLO PICASSO

Woman and Child. Barcelona, c. 1902
Conté crayon, 12⅝ x 8½″

PABLO PICASSO

El Loco. Barcelona, 1903
Watercolor, 11½ x 8¼″

PABLO PICASSO

Head of a Woman. 1903
Pastel, 11⅜ x 11⅛"

PABLO PICASSO

Man with Pack. Barcelona, 1903
Conté crayon, 12½ x 8½"

PABLO PICASSO

Woman Ironing. Paris, 1904
Oil on canvas, 45¾ x 28⅝"

PABLO PICASSO

Two Harlequins. Paris, March 26, 1905
Watercolor and gouache, 9¼ x 7″

PABLO PICASSO

Vase and Flowers. c. 1905
Ink, 10⅜ x 7¾"

PABLO PICASSO

Courtship. 1905-06

Ink, 10⅜ x 7¾"

PABLO PICASSO

Still Life: Flowers in Vase. 1905-06
Gouache on board, 27¾ x 21¼"

PABLO PICASSO

Woman with Open Fan. 1906
Ink, 6¾ x 4¼"

PABLO PICASSO

Composition. 1914-15
Gouache with pencil, 7½ x 11⅜″

PABLO PICASSO

Compotier and Musical Instruments. Paris, 1915
Watercolor and charcoal, 8¼ x 8½″

PABLO PICASSO

Three Bathers. Juan-les-Pins, August 19, 1920
Tempera and pastel, 19½ and 25⅜″

PABLO PICASSO

Saint-Servan, near Dinard. 1922
Pencil, 16⅛ x 11⅛″

61

PABLO PICASSO

The Table (Le Guéridon). December 24, 1922
Watercolor, 6½ x 4"

PABLO PICASSO

Table before the Window. 1922
Watercolor and pencil, 5½ x 4½"

63

PABLO PICASSO

Still Life with Apples. 1923
Oil with sand on canvas, 9⅜ x 12¾″

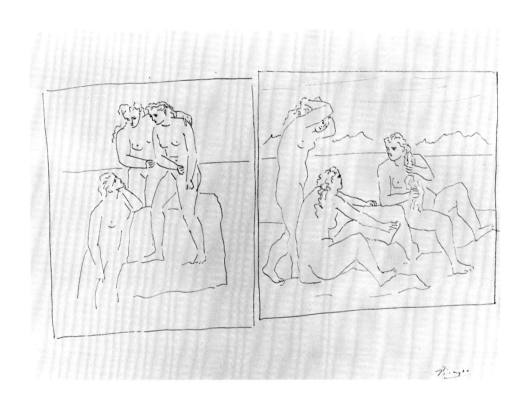

PABLO PICASSO

Two Groups of Bathers. 1923
Ink, 9⅞ x 13½"

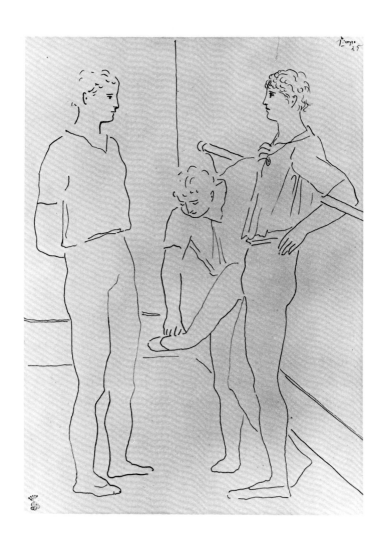

PABLO PICASSO

Three Dancers. Monte Carlo, 1925
Ink, 13⅛ x 9⅜″

PABLO PICASSO

Woman Seated. 1926
Ink, 18⅛ x 12⅛"

67

PABLO PICASSO

Bird on a Tree. Dinard, August 13, 1928

Oil on canvas, 13½ x 9¼"

PABLO PICASSO

Reclining Nude. April 3, 1929
Oil on canvas, 7¼ x 12¾″

PABLO PICASSO

Woman with Yellow Hair (Marie Thérèse Walter). December 1931-January 1932
Oil on canvas, 38⅞ x 31½"

PABLO PICASSO

Minerve (Marie Thérèse Walter). 1933
Charcoal, 10 x 12⅞"

71

PABLO PICASSO

Still Life: Fruit Dish and Pitcher. January 21, 1937
Oil on canvas, 18⅜ x 23½"

72

PABLO PICASSO

Head of a Woman (Dora Mar). 1939
Oil on wood, 23¼ x 17½"

73

PABLO PICASSO

Francoise Gilot, Juan-les-Pins, September 9, 1947
Sanguine on paper, 25 x 18⅞"

74

PABLO PICASSO

Garden in Vallauris. June 10, 1953
Oil on canvas, 7⅜ x 10½″

75

PABLO PICASSO

Houses in Vallauris. June 25, 1953
Oil on canvas, 20 x 24½"

PABLO PICASSO

Two Doves with Wings Spread. March 16, 1960
Oil on canvas, 23½ x 28¾″

1882-1963   GEORGES BRAQUE

Landscape near Antwerp. 1906

Oil on canvas, 23¾ x 32″

GEORGES BRAQUE

Teapot on Yellow Ground. November 1955
Oil on canvas, 13¾ x 25½″

79

1884-1920   AMEDEO MODIGLIANI

Caryatid. c. 1914

Oil on canvas, 39¼ x 28¾″

AMEDEO MODIGLIANI

Young Girl Seated. 1917-18
Oil on canvas, 36 x 21″

1894-1943   CHAIM SOUTINE

The Venetian. 1921-31
Oil on canvas, 31½ x 21½"

82

1884-1956 IDA FISCHER

Abstraction. c. 1945-48
Oil on canvas, 18½ x 23½″

Index

15,000 copies of this catalogue, designed by Malcolm Grear,
typeset by Craftsman Type Inc. have been printed by Eastern Press, Inc.
in April 1972 for the Trustees of The Solomon R. Guggenheim Foundation
on the occasion of the re-opening of The Justin K. Thannhauser Wing

All photographs were made by Robert E. Mates and Paul Katz